Teppanyaki
Barbecue

Teppanyaki
Barbecue

Hideo Dekura

First published in Australia in 2007 by
New Holland Publishers (Australia) Pty Ltd
Sydney • Auckland • London • Cape Town
www.newholland.com.au

1/66 Gibbes Street Chatswood NSW 2067 Australia
218 Lake Road Northcote Auckland New Zealand
86 Edgware Road London W2 2EA United Kingdom
80 McKenzie Street Cape Town 8001 South Africa

National Library of Australia Cataloguing-in-Publication Data:

Dekura, Hideo.
        Teppanyaki barbecue.

        ISBN 9781741105803 (hbk.).

        1. Barbecue cookery. 2. Cookery, Japanese. I. Title.

        641.5952

Publisher: Martin Ford
Production: Linda Bottari
Project Editor: Michael McGrath
Editor: Jenny Scepanovic
Designer: Tania Gomes
Printer: C&C printing, China

Acknowledgements

I always enjoy teaching people about Japanese cuisine. Writing a book about Japanese cuisine is a more complicated process and many people have been involved along the way. I would especially like to thank the following people for their generous help and support:

Jill Elias, for guiding me through the intricacies of English. Thanks to the Best family and their willing participation in our photography. Keiko Yoshida, for her inspirational photography and her eye for design. My kitchen assistant, Kayoko Suzuki, who worked like a Trojan with preparations for the photography. Also my dear friend Ted Takita, who always supports me.

The inspired, food-loving New Holland Publishers Australia team, Managing Director Fiona Schultz, Production Manager Linda Bottari, and Publishing Manager Martin Ford, whose enthusiasm and support has enabled my third publication with them to come to fruition.

Finally to all those who have supplied equipment, provisions and their constant support over the years:

Kikkoman Australia
Colza, Teppanyaki restaurant, Tokyo, Japan
Japan Food Corporation
Nikon Cameras Australia
Sydney Fish Markets
Kirin Beer Australia
Wheel and Barrow Australia
Meat and Livestock Australia
Barbeques Galore Australia

Contents

Teppanyaki

鉄板焼の楽しみ方

Teppanyaki:
Versatile and Entertaining

Teppanyaki is a traditional Japanese method of cooking seafood, meat and vegetables on a hotplate. The word derives from two words: 'teppan' meaning iron pan, and 'yaki' meaning to grill.

Teppanyaki evolved in post World War II Kyoto when displaced people collected scrap metal from the debris and used it over open fires to cook their food. I have fond childhood memories of helping prepare the charcoal for the hibachi or kanteki (clay pot) at dinnertime, chatting with my mother while she cooked the himono (dried seafood), sanma, (autumn blue fish), yellowtail fish, and the readily available fresh baby eggplants (aubergines) and shishitou (Japanese green chilli) on the wire mesh ami of the hibachi. It was a real treat to have beef marinated in miso, though chicken was often available because people kept them for eggs. Somewhere along the way, teppanyaki took on a more dignified style; however, it retains some of its original simplicity and the cook's sense of being at one with the food.

Many Westerners have become familiar with the term through the prevalence of Teppanyaki restaurants, where diners can watch their meal being cooked on hotplates, usually with a dexterous juggling and manipulation of food and utensils, accompanied by sometimes breathtaking performances of culinary acrobatics. However, in Japan, Teppanyaki restaurants are usually much more sedate affairs; casual or formal, yet still featuring the skill and agility of the chef as he or she cooks and serves the food.

In this book I have no intention of teaching or encouraging such a dramatic style of teppanyaki, rather I wish to introduce you to a Japanese style of cooking that can be readily adapted to the ever-popular Western style of barbecuing. It is a style of cooking that is quick and easy, and incorporates the cook as an integral part of the whole dining process, rather than relegating him or her to the kitchen or the barbecue.

The food is cooked where it is to be eaten, and the diners are involved by their presence and interaction in the process, making the meal a very convivial experience. The cook's sensitivity to the ingredients, the preparation and a polished style of cooking and serving are the essentials of teppanyaki, and the elements which distinguish it from the traditional Western-style barbecue. Teppanyaki is an easy, tasty alternative for those who are seeking a change from steaks and sausages.

Teppanyaki is usually cooked on a steel hotplate. You can cook most of the recipes in this book on an outdoor barbecue; however, it is not always possible for diners to sit in the near vicinity of a barbecue. Fortunately, you can now buy electric teppanyaki hotplates from electrical appliance shops, which can be used both indoors and out. If you don't have a teppanyaki hotplate or an outdoor barbecue, you can just as easily use an electric frying pan to cook teppanyaki dishes at the table. Some of the dishes are suitable for cooking on an hibachi, a traditional Japanese charcoal brazier, which you can purchase from a barbecue shop, and sometimes a mesh grill known as an 'amiyaki' is used instead of the hotplate. Throughout the book I tell you which recipes are suitable for cooking on a hotplate and which are suitable for an hibachi or mesh grill.

In teppanyaki restaurants, the chef may pluck sea creatures from a nearby water tank, then slice and cook them in front of the waiting diners. At home, we don't have this luxury, but teppanyaki provides the perfect opportunity to serve delicious seafood dishes in a very short time. Meats such as beef, pork and chicken, and many fresh, seasonal vegetables can be cut into bite-sized pieces and grilled in this style. The ingredients may be marinated beforehand or served with a variety of dipping sauces. The usual accompaniments are steamed or fried rice, salads, pickles, miso soup and other side dishes.

The teppanyaki hotplate, or teppan, is a versatile piece of equipment that can be used to cook a range of other dishes as well. One of these is okonomiyaki, a very popular meal originating in Osaka and Hiroshima. In Japan it is often available from street vendors cooking on a portable teppan, and the sweet, savoury smell of the okonomiyaki sauce wafting through the air is enough to tempt anyone's tastebuds. The basic ingredients are egg and cabbage, but there are many variations of this tasty Japanese-style pancake. Another all-time favourite, yakisoba, or noodles, is also cooked on the teppan. The unique flavour of the yakisoba sauce distinguishes this dish from all other stir-fried noodles.

Whether teppanyaki is eaten in a restaurant or at home, one of its essential features, which adds to the overall enjoyment, is the entertaining way the food is cooked and served to waiting diners—very relaxing, yet stimulating. Seeing the fresh food, watching someone cooking and smelling the delicious aromas is sure to whet the appetite. It's a similar experience to sitting at a sushi bar, or even a sushi train restaurant, where watching the cook deftly handling the ingredients is a source of fascination and temptation.

This display creates a certain atmosphere and is suited to the Japanese style of dining, where it is usual for food to be served in a series of smaller, separate portions, sometimes not much more than a mouthful that can be savoured to the fullest.

Teppanyaki barbecuing is not just about the necessity of eating food, but is a social event, combining the enjoyment of eating with conversation, and maybe a bit of entertainment thrown in for good measure.

In this book, I introduce you to the basic idea of teppanyaki, using standard ingredients and techniques. I hope that after reading it and following the recipes you will feel confident to experiment, using a variety of ingredients and sauces, because the possibilities of teppanyaki are really limitless once you understand the basic principles.

Indoor Teppanyaki

In Japan, there are a number of traditional dishes that involve a continual process of cooking and eating, such as sukiyaki or nabe (hot pot). Teppanyaki, using an electric teppanyaki hotplate (or electric frying pan) is a similar experience. Most of the preparation is done beforehand, and the cooking begins when all the company are seated round the table. Diners watch the chef as he or she barbecues, and sample small amounts of tasty delights as they are cooked and served. Naturally, at home there is not a chef in the same way there is at a restaurant, so the diners should not be expecting a grand performance, but this style of cooking does afford the host the opportunity to show off their cooking skills and knowledge of ingredients. Most importantly, the cook and diners share the cooking and eating experience together.

Here are some menu suggestions.

Menu 1

Tomato and Daikon Salad with Dashi Dressing (see page 138)

Okonomiyaki (Osaka- or Hiroshima-style (see page 144 or 148)

Yakisoba or Yakiudon (see page 153 or 150)

Sorbets (see page 170)

In Japan it is common for okonomiyaki to be served with beer, but it is also served with shouchu, on the rocks, mixed with cold or hot water, or soda water, and served with citrus. Shouchu is a distilled spirit made mainly from sweet potato, common potato, barley or buckwheat. It may contain up to 45 per cent alcohol.

Menu 2

Green Salad (see page 30)

Yakiniku (see page 36)

Fried Rice (see page 163)

Grilled Seasonal Fruits (see page 169)

Teppan Party Outdoors

The beauty of teppanyaki barbecuing is its adaptability. You can cook on a small electric teppanyaki hotplate indoors, but it is also suitable for cooking on larger barbecue hotplates outdoors and even in picnic areas. As with any barbecue, you need to plan carefully for the number of people to be catered for, prepare all the ingredients in advance, and have good equipment and a clean hotplate. However, it is fun to bring some more exciting tastes to the outdoor barbecue, and create a more exotic atmosphere. Open space allows the teppanyaki cook more room to be dramatic if desired. It is important to work neatly and precisely when cooking and serving.

Menu
Butterfly King Prawns or Crispy King Prawns (shrimp) (see pages 107 and 105)
Steak with Teriyaki Sauce and Green Salad (see page 30)
Oysters with Green Tea Miso Meringues (see page 114)
Ice-cream Crepes (see page 174)

Amiyaki

Amiyaki is the Japanese method of barbecuing on an open mesh, which is similar to the Western concept of cooking on a barbecue. The open mesh allows the fats and juices to drip onto the hot coals below, creating a tempting aroma, and the wafting smoke adds to the flavour.

The hibachi, a traditional Japanese charcoal brazier, was the main source of heat in the cold season before gas and kerosene heaters were introduced in Japan. They are used for both heating and cooking, and come in a variety of sizes and designs. A large hibachi may be set in the centre of a table, and is a cosy way to heat a room and cook a meal for family and friends. The smaller portable hibachi is commonly used as an interior brazier in homes and is often seen in ryokan (Japanese inns) or restaurants.

You can buy an hibachi from kitchenware shops or hardware shops in Japan. Japanese hibachis usually have a ceramic or clay base to contain the hot charcoal, whereas Western versions are made of cast iron. You can use the grill on your outdoor barbecue for the recipes that use an hibachi—buy the mesh from Japanese or Asian shops to place over your barbecue. Slate can be used as an alternative.

One type of clay hibachi is the shichirin, which has a very deep base to contain the charcoal. Even though we had gas in our kitchen, my mother used the shichirin to do slow cooking and grilling. I still remember sitting beside the pot and helping her by fanning the fish with an uchiwa (Japanese fan), the wonderful smell of fish and beans cooking remains with me to this day. Make sure the room is well ventilated when you use an hibachi inside a house.

Menu

Eggplant (Aubergine) Amiyaki (see page 134)
Whiting with Green Tea Salt (see page 99)
Chicken Yakitori (see page 62)
Grilled Eel (see page 76)
Fried Rice (see page 163)

Teppanyaki Tools

Carving fork: Used to hold meat when cutting on the teppan.

Electric teppanyaki hotplate: Iron or stainless steel plate for cooking on; use an electric frying pan or outdoor barbecue hotplate if you don't have one.

Hibachi: Charcoal brazier; cooking is done on an open mesh. Use an outdoor barbecue if you don't have one.

Knives: Sharp carving knives are useful for slicing meats and seafood.

Ladle: A ladle with a lip is particularly useful for pouring sauces and liquids.

Metal spatula: Useful when making okonomiyaki and teppanyaki. Available in a variety of sizes.

Oil spreader: Used to spread oil evenly on the pan. Available from Japanese or Asian shops.

Pepper and salt mills: Freshly ground pepper and salt enhance the flavours.

Scrapers: Angled or straight, used for turning and cutting food. Avoid using stainless steel scrapers on Teflon plates.

Tongs: Essential utensils unless you are good at using chopsticks, in which case you may use long cooking chopsticks.

Teppanyaki Shopping List

amiyaki	mesh grill	**sake**	rice wine
abura age	fried bean curd	**sakura ebi**	dried pink shrimps
aonori	dried green seaweed (flakes or powder)	**sansho**	Japanese mountain pepper
bainiku/umeboshi	pickled plum puree	**shichimi**	Japanese seven spices
benishoga	red pickled ginger	**shiitake**	shiitake mushroom
bonito flakes	dried bonito (fish) flakes	**shimji**	shimji mushroom
cyuzu	citrus	**shishitou**	Japanese green chilli
daikon	white radish	**shiso**	Japanese green basil
dashi	Japanese stock	**tenkasu**	deep-fried tempura butter drops
enoki	enoki mushroom		
hibachi	charcoal griller	**teppan**	iron hotplate/pan
katakuriko	potato starch	**udon**	udon noodle
katsuo bushi	dried bonito flakes	**umeboshi**	pickled plum
katsuo dashi	bonito stock	**wagyu**	Japanese beef
kuzu powder	Japanese mountain potato starch	**wasabi**	Japanese green horse radish
mirin	sweet cooking sake	**white miso paste**	soy bean paste
miso	soy bean paste	**yakiniku**	grill beef on teppan or open mesh
mizuna leaves	peppery lettuce		
nerigoma	white or black sesame paste	**porkyamaimo**	Japanese mountain yam
		yamaimo	yam potato
okonomiyaki	Japanese savoury pancake	**yukari**	dried red shiso, Japanese red basil powder
ponzu	Japanese citrus vinaigrette	**yuzu**	Japanese citrus

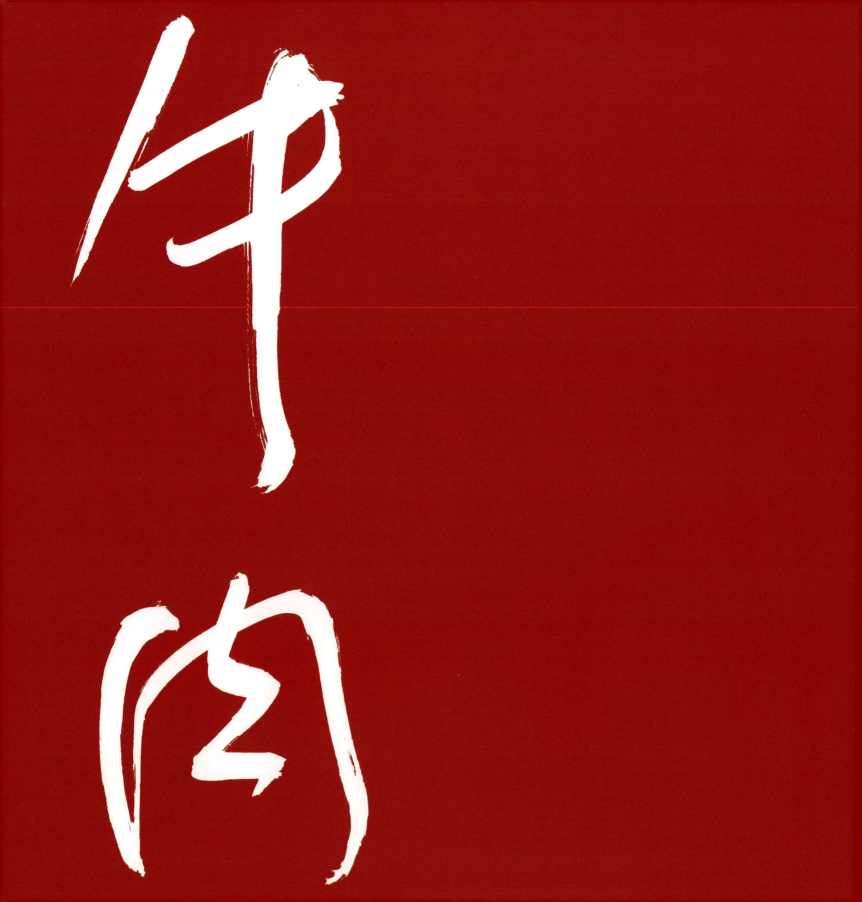

Beef

Beef

Teppanyaki is a quick method of cooking, so tender cuts of beef are essential. Apart from selecting particular cuts, it is difficult to judge whether meat is tender. Follow your butcher's advice if you are lucky enough to have a good one.

Sirloin is fine for all teppanyaki dishes, including amiyaki and marinated meat dishes. Rib roast is also suitable, as it is tender and usually has a reasonable amount of marbling—the small white flecks of fat in the beef. Marbling enhances the eating quality of beef by increasing the tenderness, juiciness and flavour. Tenderloin is also suitable, but more delicate and Japanese chefs often prefer to cook it over a mild heat—even in a frying pan on top of the teppan—rather than the usual method of searing sirloin on a high heat on each side, then lowering the heat. You can use rump steak, which, although it does not contain much marbling, is usually moderately priced, the texture is fine and it is reasonably tender.

In Japan, the preferred beef is wagyu. This literally translates to 'Japanese beef', but refers to beef from cattle that are raised under very strict conditions, only in Japan. Similar beef from cross-breeds has become available in other countries, and is even being imported by Japan. Wagyu is expensive and characterised by a large degree of marbelling, which results in a tenderness and richness of flavour not found in regular beef.

Whatever the differences between Japanese and Western cooking styles, both agree that steak is very tasty when cooked on a hotplate. There are many types of steak and many cooking methods, but they all stimulate the appetite and tempt the tastebuds when the aroma wafts through the air as the meat hits the hotplate, especially when wagyu is used.

Professional teppanyaki chefs cook wagyu on a 2.5 cm (1in) thick hotplate. Because the plate is so thick, the heat builds up evenly and creates a very crispy outer coating when heavily marbled meat is seared to seal in the juices and flavour. When the heat is reduced by pouring on wine and covering with a lid to steam, the steak retains its richness.Wagyu has such a beautiful, rich flavour, that it can be enjoyed without seasoning or sauces. Simply cook and serve it on its own.

Steak with Teriyaki Sauce and Green Salad

Serves 4

vegetable oil for cooking
800g (1½lb) wagyu sirloin or sirloin (200g/7oz per person), trimmed
4 fresh green shishitou chillis, de-seeded and halved
salt to taste
¼ cup teriyaki sauce (page 183)

Green Salad

iceberg lettuce, cut in half, or other
green salad leaves, rinsed and dried
1 tomato, diced or cut into wedges
½ Lebanese cucumber, sliced diagonally
2 red radishes, rinsed and thinly sliced

Dressing

3 tablespoons rice vinegar
3 tablespoons soy sauce
1 teaspoon sugar
3 tablespoons vegetable oil
lime or lemon juice to taste

Prepare salad first. Tear lettuce into bite-sized pieces. Combine with tomato, cucumber and radishes in a serving bowl. Mix all dressing ingredients together and whisk well. Drizzle over salad.

Heat a teppan, electric frying pan or barbecue hotplate and brush or spray with oil. Grill both sides of steak to seal in the flavour, cooking for about 2 minutes before turning.

At the same time, cook chilli on the edge of the hotplate. Brush teriyaki sauce over both sides of the meat and cook to your preference. Drizzle teriyaki sauce over the chilli and cook until soft.

Slice meat on the teppan into bite-sized pieces. Arrange beef with chilli on individual plates.

Shishitou chillis are not particularly hot. If you prefer hot chilli, use a red variety. Use gloves when handling chillis. Add any of the following for variety and a stronger taste: wasabi paste, crushed garlic, grated green ginger, chilli or sesame oil.

Cubed Steak

Serves 4

400g (14oz) rump steak
vegetable oil for cooking
¼ bunch chives, chopped
¼ cup grated daikon
a bowl of iced water for resting the meat
ponzu (see page 181)

Trim steak and slice into four 2.5–3 cm (1–1½in) thick strips
Heat a teppan, electric frying pan or barbecue hotplate and spread with oil.Sear strips on all
four sides, approximately 2 minutes each side.
Place the meat into the iced water to cool.
Wipe the excess water off the meat with a paper towel.
Slice each strip into cubes.
Serve with ponzu and grated daikon. Garnish with chives.

Grate daikon with a cheese grater or Japanese-style grater.

Chuck Rib on Amiyaki

Serves 4

500g (1lb) chuck rib or short rib, chopped approximately 3 x 25cm (1½ x 9½in) including the bone, into 4 pieces
2 brown onions, peeled and sliced
1 carrot, peeled and sliced diagonally
4 shishitou or capsicum (sweet peppers), cut in half and de-seeded
yakiniku sauce (see page 184)

Marinate ribs in yakiniku sauce for 30 minutes

Prepare hibachi (Japanese charcoal brazier) with charcoal, and place mesh on top. Grill vegetables on the edge of the mesh where the heat is lower, and grill the ribs in the centre.

Occasionally brush yakiniku sauce over the ribs. When the ribs are cooked, cut into bite-sized pieces using cooking scissors. Sprinkle salt over the vegetables if desired and serve with the meat.

When you purchase the beef, ask the butcher to cut it for you.
This cut of beef is readily available from Asian butchers.
Yakiniku sauce can also be bought from Japanese or Asian grocery shops.

Yakiniku

Serves 4

400g (14oz) topside or rump, sliced (approximately 5 x 7cm/2 x 2½in slices)
8 fresh shiitake mushrooms, trimmed
½ green capsicum, de-seeded and sliced (2 x 2cm/¾ x ¾in slices)
1 carrot, peeled and sliced
1 bunch asparagus, trimmed
1 brown onion, peeled and sliced in rings
200g (7oz) cabbage, rinsed and sliced (2 x 2cm/¾ x ¾in slices)
1 eggplant (aubergine), sliced
vegetable oil or beef fat
yakiniku sauce (page 184)
Japanese mayonnaise
cooked rice

Prepare all ingredients on a large plate.

Heat a teppan, electric frying pan or barbecue hotplate and spread with oil or beef fat.

Grill all ingredients, removing when each item is done, and serve in individual bowls with rice and yakiniku sauce or Japanese mayonnaise.

Beer is a good accompaniment for yakiniku. In Japan, a popular trend is
to eat yakiniku served wrapped in an iceberg lettuce leaf.
The beef can be marinated in yakiniku sauce before grilling.
Other cuts of beef such as sirloin or tenderloin, or offal (liver or kidneys) can be used.
Alternative vegetables are bean sprouts, pumpkin (parboiled) and shishitou.

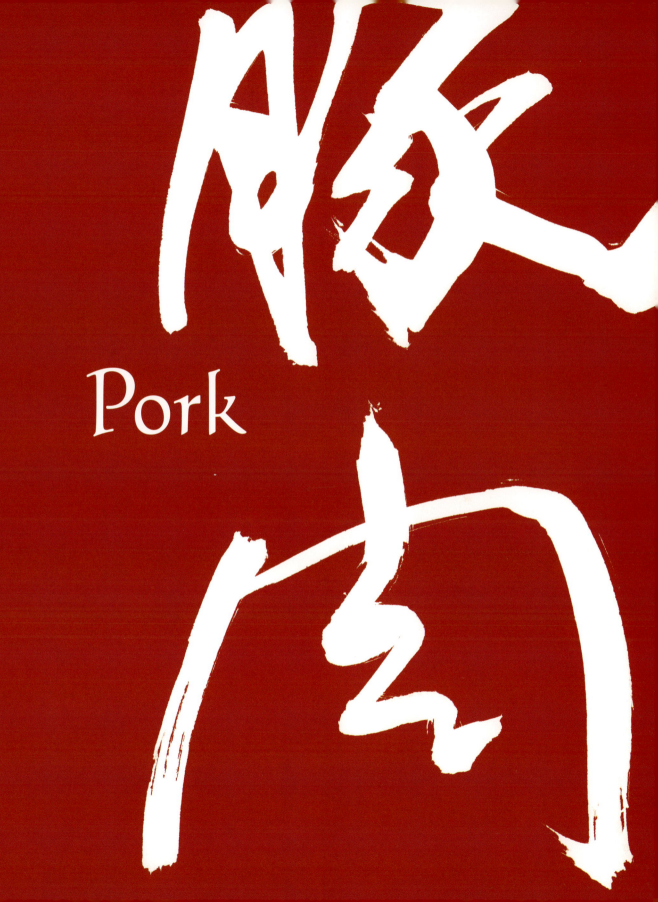

Pork

Pork

Pork is often used in modern Japanese cooking. Although thinly sliced pork is commonly used, cuts containing more fat are also popular. Japanese people tend to prefer the flavour of pork and beef with some fat. The fat content in pork and wagyu dishes may not be considered particularly healthy, but since these dishes are not consumed frequently or in large amounts, it may not be too detrimental to one's health.

Crispy Pork

Serves 4

2 tablespoons mirin
2 tablespoons balsamic vinegar
400g (14oz) lean pork
2 tablespoons potato starch, kuzu powder or katakuriko
2 tablespoons butter
1 teaspoon chopped garlic
4 sundried tomatoes, chopped
2 tablespoons breadcrumbs
2 tablespoons chopped parsley
1 tablespoon butter for grilling
1 pinch salt
toothpicks

Mix together mirin and balsamic vinegar.

Thinly slice the pork. Roll up each slice of pork and fasten with a toothpick. Coat the pork rolls with potato starch.

Heat the teppanyaki hotplate, electric frying pan or barbecue hotplate and add butter.

Grill the rolls. When cooked, transfer onto the chopping board, and slice in half.

Place the rolls on an oven tray. Sprinkle with the mirin and balsamic vinegar mixture. Top with garlic and dried tomato. Grill for one minute.

Remove from griller and sprinkle with breadcrumbs, parsley and butter, then put back under the grill until breadcrumbs turn golden brown. Garnish with fresh parsley to serve.

Asparagus Pork Rolls

Serves 4

200g (7oz) thinly sliced pork
8 asparagus stalks, trimmed and blanched
3 tablespoons potato starch, kuzu powder or katakuriko
1 tablespoon vegetable oil
teriyaki sauce (see page 183), kept hot in a saucepan
toothpicks

Divide the pork into equal amounts of 8 and roll up each asparagus stalk tightly with one or two strips of meat. Coat the rolls with potato starch, and secure with toothpicks to tighten the rolls. Heat a teppan, electric frying pan or barbecue hotplate and spread evenly with oil.

Cook the rolls thoroughly on the hotplate. Place the rolls in the warm teriyaki sauce in the saucepan and leave for a while.

Take out the rolls and slice into bite-sized pieces.

This kind of pork is available from Asian
butchers and some Asian grocers.

Diced Pork Steak

Serves 4

¼ cup tomato sauce

1 teaspoon Japanese or English mustard

2 tablespoons caster sugar

2 tablespoons mirin

vegetable oil

400g (14oz) pork rump or pork loin steak with fat left on (preferably 5cm/2in thick), cut into quarters

60ml (2fl oz) sake or white wine

1 brown onion, peeled and sliced in rings

black pepper to taste

8 pistachio nuts, crushed

4 mint leaves

Mix together tomato sauce, mustard, caster sugar and mirin. Set aside.

Heat a teppan, electric frying pan or barbecue hotplate and spread evenly with oil. Brown pork on all sides.

Sprinkle with sake or white wine and cover with the lid to steam for 1–2 minutes.

Cook onion on teppan beside the steaks, stirring well. Pour the tomato sauce mixture over the steaks and combine with onion.

Sprinkle black pepper and pistachio nuts over the top of the meat.

Serve on individual plates garnished with mint leaves

Pork with Ginger Teriyaki Sauce

Serves 4

1 cup teriyaki sauce (see page 183)
1 tablespoon ginger juice (made by squeezing grated fresh ginger)
200g (7oz) pork loin, sliced or thinly sliced pork
2 cups cabbage, thinly sliced (use a slicer or mandolin if available) and soaked in water
1 handful snow pea (sugar pea) sprouts
1 tomato, cut into wedges
vegetable oil

Prepare teriyaki sauce and stir in ginger juice.

With a knife, make several slits in the pork to avoid shrinking. Marinate pork in the teriyaki sauce and ginger for at least 30 minutes in the refrigerator.

To prepare salad, drain cabbage and mix with sprouts. Place salad and tomato on the side of four serving plates.

Heat a teppan, electric frying pan or barbecue hotplate and spread evenly with oil. Drain off excess marinade and cook pork over medium heat.

Serve with salad.

This kind of pork is available from Asian butchers or grocers.

Lamb

Lamb

Lamb is not as popular as beef or pork in Japan, except in Hokkaido, the northern island of Japan. The characteristic flavour of lamb tends to be considered too strong by many Japanese. However, since the introduction of Jingisukan—one of Hokkaido's regional dishes—into other areas of Japan, lamb is slowly gaining popularity.

Jingisukan (the Japanese word for Genghis Khan), a barbecued lamb dish, is typical of the regional cuisine in Hokkaido. There are two methods of cooking: one is to grill sliced lamb marinated in a special sauce and the other is to grill lamb slices and serve with the sauce.

Jingisukan

In Jingisukan, a special dome-shaped hotplate—like a turtle's shell is used to prevent the oil and sauces from pooling and stewing the meat while it's grilling. Jingisukan can be cooked at home with a Jingisukan plate—bought from Asian shops—on a portable gas or electric hotplate at the dining table. This Jingisukan dish has a combination of vegetables and marinated lamb that is meant to be eaten as it is being cooked, so set the hotplate up at the dining table

Serves 4

Jingisukan (Genghis Khan) sauce (see page 185)
400g (14oz) lamb rump, thinly sliced
small cube of lamb fat, or vegetable oil
1 packet of bean sprouts, rinsed and drained
garlic chives, chopped, added to bean sprouts
1 brown onion, peeled and sliced in rings
1 carrot, peeled, sliced and precooked in microwave
1 green capsicum (sweet peppers), de-seeded and cut into pieces
any other vegetable in season, such as cabbage, pumpkin, snow peas (sugar peas), etc.

Marinate lamb in prepared sauce for at least half an hour. Heat the dome-shaped teppan and spread with lamb fat or oil. Place some bean sprouts with chives, onion, carrot and capsicum on the teppan. Grill for 2–3 minutes or until lightly cooked.

Place some lamb slices on the hotplate and cook for 2–3 minutes, turning once. Drizzle some sauce over the vegetables.

You can eat directly from the dome teppan, continuing to add more ingredients to the hotplate as required. Serve with Jinisukan sauce for dipping.

Lamb with Green Seaweed

Serves 4

400g (14oz) lamb fillet
4 tablespoons sake
8 fresh shiitake or nameko mushrooms
2 tablespoons butter
1 tablespoon mirin
2 tablespoons soy sauce
3 tablespoons aonori

Trim lamb and cut into 4 x 100g (3½oz) pieces.

To butterfly the lamb, using a sharp knife partially slice through each piece of meat, stopping 1cm (0.5in) from the edge. Score meat at 1cm intervals on one side.

Sprinkle sake over the lamb.

Heat a teppan, electric frying pan or barbecue hotplate and spread with butter. Cook the lamb as preferred. At the same time, on one side of the plate place mushrooms and stir.

Combine mirin and soy sauce, sprinkle over the lamb while cooking.

Sprinkle aonori over the lamb.

Chicken

Chicken

Chicken is a popular ingredient in Japanese cooking because of the stability of price and its great affinity with Japanese soy sauce, which has a hint of sweetness. The smell of grilled chicken with soy sauce always makes my mouth water.

Teriyaki sauce with a touch of ginger also brings out the flavour of any cut of chicken.

Yakitori literally means grilled chicken, which may be done using either the teppanyaki or amiyaki method. Yakitori is a very popular dish not only when cooked at home but also in Japanese pubs known as 'izakaya', where portions of chicken are grilled on the teppan and served with teriyaki sauce or salt. There are also many small restaurants specialising in yakitori.

Chicken Yakitori

Yakitori is skewered chicken, flavoured with teriyaki sauce or salt, grilled over a charcoal fire.

Serves 4

200g (7oz) thigh fillet, trimmed and cut into bite-sized cubes
200g (7oz) chicken livers, trimmed and cut into bite-sized cubes
4 stems spring onion, thick stems, trimmed and cut into 3cm (1¼in) lengths
teriyaki sauce (see page 183)
sea salt to taste
bamboo skewers

Thread chicken, chicken livers and spring onions onto bamboo skewers. For a strong teriyaki flavour, marinate skewered chicken for at least 30 minutes.

Grill under the griller, or barbecue on the open teppan, hibachi or barbecue hotplate, turning often until cooked, occasionally brushing with sauce. Serve hot.

You can substitute shishitou for the spring onion if you prefer.
For salted yakitori, sprinkle with salt over the chicken and grill.

Kneaded Chicken Tsukune

Makes 12 pieces

400g (14oz) chicken mince
50g (1½oz) frozen yamaimo potato or 15g (½oz) yamaimo powder
dissolved in 1 tablespoon water
1 egg
2 tablespoons potato starch or kuzu powder or katakuriko
1 small piece green ginger, peeled
1 stem spring onion, chopped
extra potato starch for coating
1 tablespoon olive oil
12 disposable chopsticks, cut to about 5cm (2in) long

Sweet and Hot Sauce

2 tablespoons light coloured soy sauce
1 tablespoon fresh red chilli, de-seeded and chopped
½ cup cold water
2 tablespoons caster sugar
2 tablespoons mirin
1 lemon, zest and juice

To make sweet and hot sauce, mix all ingredients except lemon zest in a pan. Cook over medium heat stirring occasionally until mixture thickens slightly. Add lemon zest and stir, then remove from heat.

Using a food processor, whiz chicken mince and yamaimo until smooth. Break egg into processor, add ginger and potato starch, then whiz again.

Transfer to a bowl, add spring onion, and combine well. Pat potato starch over your hands and form the chicken mixture into 12 balls

Skewer each ball with a chopstick, then press carefully with your hand to flatten. Set for 15 minutes in the refrigerator.

Heat a teppan, electric frying pan or barbecue hotplate and spread with oil. Grill skewered chicken on both sides.

Brush with sweet and hot sauce and grill until cooked through. Serve hot.

You can sometimes find fresh yamaimo potato in Japanese or Asian grocers.

Fish

Fish

It is important to have very fresh fish for teppanyaki. When purchasing a whole fish, make sure it has clear eyes. If you're able to touch the fish, feel that the flesh is firm and check that the gills are a reddish colour. Also, if the fish is not gutted, check that the belly side is firm, not ruptured or discoloured. If it has a brownish tinge underneath, it is not fresh. If the fish has been gutted, the internal cavity should be clean, but have traces of blood along the spine. The smell of fish is another indicator of its freshness, as old fish has an unpleasant odour.

It is harder to choose fresh fish fillets, but the qualities you should check for are a bright colour, firm texture of the flesh and a pleasant 'sea' smell that is not too strong.

When grilling a fish with scales, such as a snapper, I prefer to grill it with the scales on to seal in the flavour.

Bonito Tataki

Serves 4

400g (14oz) bonito fillet, with skin on
(if bonito is unavailable, use salmon)
2 tablespoons sea salt
2 tablespoons sake
cooking spray
2 tablespoons soy sauce
1 tablespoon wasabi paste
bowl of iced water
3 metal skewers

Topping

2 cloves garlic, chopped
½ cup rice vinegar
80g caster sugar
1 brown onion, peeled and sliced into rings
2 stems spring onion, trimmed and chopped
50g (1½oz) green ginger, peeled and shredded

To make topping mixture, combine garlic, rice vinegar and sugar in a bowl. Then add onion, spring onion and ginger, then toss. Set aside until use.

With a pair of tweezers, remove bones from bonito fillet. Insert metal skewers at even intervals through the flesh just under the skin.

Sprinkle sake on both sides of the bonito.

Sprinkle with salt over the skin side only.

Grill the fish skin-side down under the heated barbecue hot plate for a couple of minutes. Cook fillet for 2 minutes. Place the fillet in a bowl of iced water to cool down.

Take out the bonito and pat dry with paper towel. Remove the skewers.

Cut fillet into 0.5cm (0.2in) thick slices.

Serve on a plate and cover with topping, soy sauce and wasabi paste.

Dried Anchovies

Serves 4

  1 tablespoon soy sauce
  1 tablespoon mirin
  1 teaspoon caster sugar
  100g (3½oz) dried anchovies
  1 teaspoon white sesame
  1 teaspoon sesame seed oil

Mix soy sauce, mirin and sugar in a small saucepan and warm.

Shake anchovies in a sieve to remove loose flakes.

Put anchovies and white sesame seeds on a heated teppan, electric frying pan or barbecue hotplate and stir well while roasting.

Add sesame oil and stir. Pour soy sauce mixture over anchovies and cook for 2 minutes.

Serve hot.

Dried anchovies are available from Asian or Japanese grocers.
You can add dried chili powder or shichimi (Japanese seven spice) to make spicy dried anchovies.
These are good nibbles to have with beer or sake.

Grilled Eel

Serves 4

2 short black fin eels
bamboo skewers

Sauce

bones and head left over from filleted eels
1/3 cup rock sugar
1/4 cup soy sauce
1 teaspoon sansho pepper
120ml (4oz) water
60ml (2oz) sake
60ml (2oz) mirin

Eels are slippery and difficult to fillet in one piece. It is better to chop eel into 15cm (6in) portions, and then insert a knife along the centre bone to butterfly and remove gut.

To make the sauce, put the head, tail and trimmings from filleted eels, along with other sauce ingredients in a pan. Bring to the boil, and cook over a low heat for 30 minutes.

Thread 2 skewers through each piece of eel, just under the skin, at right angles to the spine, 1cm (½in) in from the edge

Grill eel over an hibachi or barbecue hotplate, occasionally brushing with sauce. Alternatively dip the pieces of eel into the sauce in the pan several times while grilling—the colour of the flesh will turn opaque white when it is done. Serve with extra sauce.

Short black fin eels are available at large fishmongers or Asian fishmongers.
Do not use the larger varieties.

Flounder with Tarragon

Serves 4

   4 flounders
   salt to taste
   1 vegetable oil
   2 tablespoons butter
   2 tablespoons white wine
   2 tablespoons dry tarragon flakes
   1 lime, wedges

Scale and rinse the fish. Make a slit in the belly and remove the guts and gills, then rinse again.

On the side with the eyes, score the thick part of the fish and sprinkle with salt.

Heat a teppan, electric frying pan or barbecue hotplate and spread evenly with oil. Place flounders scored-side down and grill for 2 minutes, then turn and cook the other side.

Spread the butter on each fish then sprinkle with white wine and tarragon flakes.

Cover with lid and steam for about 3 minutes.

Serve on a plate with lime wedges.

Garfish with Plum Paste

Serves 4

8 garfish
2 hard-boiled egg yolks, sieved or mashed
100g (3½oz) cheddar cheese, thinly sliced
8 pieces English spinach, blanched
2 tablespoons umeboshi or bainiku
2 tablespoons olive oil
toothpicks

To prepare garfish, cut off the head, insert a knife into the belly side to make a slit and then open up like a butterfly. Gut and rinse under running water.

Place spinach and cheddar cheese inside the belly and secure firmly with a toothpick. Repeat for each fish.

Heat a teppan, electric frying pan or barbecue hotplate and spread evenly with oil. Place garfish on hotplate and cook both sides gently.

Place on a serving plate, sprinkle with egg and serve with plum paste on the side.

Hiramasa King Fish with Sea Salt

Serves 4

4 x 100g (3½oz) hiramasa king fish cutlets, with skin on

2 tablespoons mirin

sea salt to taste

50g (1½oz) green ginger, peeled and cut into long, needle-thin strips

4 tablespoons grated daikon radish

4 fennel fronds

4 toothpicks

2 tablespoons soy sauce

Place king fish cutlets on a tray and sprinkle with mirin and salt. Using toothpicks, secure the belly side closed.

Place cutlets on an hibachi or barbecue hotplate and grill both sides, using tongs, spatula or chopsticks to gently turn the fish.

When cooked, serve on a plate and garnish with ginger, fennel and daikon radish. Serve soy sauce as a dipping sauce on the side.

Silver Bream with Yuzu Chilli

Serves 4

4 silver bream or snapper (300g each)
4 tablespoons sake
¼ cup salt
cooking spray
4 lemon wedges

1 teaspoon yuzu powder or chopped lemon zest
1 teaspoon shichimi powder
2 tablespoons aonori
4 tablespoons soy sauce
8 metal skewers

Gut fish, leave heads and scales on. Using 2 skewers per fish, thread the first skewer diagonally across the fish, piercing the fish above the mouth to below the tail. Push the second skewer through below the mouth to above the tail, making the fish arch in the middle where the skewers cross. Sprinkle sake and salt on each fish.

Spray oil over the fish and place under the heated grill, skewer-side down, until crisp—about 5 minutes. Fish should be served with this side facing upwards, so it is important that it is nicely coloured on this side. Turn and cook arched side.

Transfer fish from grill to serving plate, skewer side up. Using kitchen glove or tea towel to hold the fish, carefully remove the skewers, giving a slight twist if they do not slide out easily.

Serve with lemon wedges. Sprinkle with yuzu and shichimi powder and green nori flakes. Serve soy sauce as a dipping sauce on the side.

When eating, remove skin and scales together.
Grilling fish with the scales prevents the flavour from being lost.

Salmon Cappuccino

Serves 4

½ cup milk
1 chicken stock cube
½ egg white
salt and ground black pepper to taste
400g (14oz) salmon fillet, cut into 4 x 100g (3½oz) portions
2 tablespoons butter
8 cocktail (grape) tomatoes, scored with a cross
2 stems spring onion, trimmed, shredded and soaked in water

Warm milk in a pan and add chicken stock cube, whisk well. Add egg white and whisk. Set aside.

Sprinkle salt and pepper over salmon.

Heat a teppan, electric frying pan or barbecue hotplate and spread with butter. Cook salmon on both sides.

Serve on a plate with tomatoes and top with whisked milk froth and shredded spring onion.

Salmon Chan-Chan Yaki

Hokkaido, the northern island of Japan, is well known for its long cold winters and its abundant supplies of natural resources from the ocean, in particular the salmon. One of its regional dishes using salmon is salmon chan-chan yaki—steamed salmon in miso paste. There is some conjecture about the meaning of this dish's name. One idea is that it is father's dish, the word 'chan' meaning 'father' in colloquial old Japanese. Another is that chan-chan represents the sound being made by chopsticks tapping against the side of the bowl or teppan by the waiting diners.

Serves 4

1 tablespoon vegetable oil or butter

2 brown onions, peeled and sliced

1 carrot, peeled and cut in julienne strips

4 x 200g (7oz) salmon fillets

1 packet bean sprouts, soaked in water and drained

4 stems spring onion, cut diagonally 4–3cm

2 tablespoons butter

Miso Chan-Chan

2 tablespoons white miso paste

2 tablespoons red miso paste

1 tablespoon soy sauce

1 tablespoon sake

1 tablespoon mirin

1 teaspoon caster sugar

2 garlic cloves, grated

sesame oil and chilli paste for extra flavour, if desired

To make miso chan-chan, combine all ingredients and mix well. Set aside.

Heat a teppan, electric frying pan or barbecue hotplate, drop on oil, and stir onion and carrot over a low heat for 2–3 minutes.

Lightly season salmon fillets with salt and pepper. Place salmon on top of the vegetables.

Top with bean sprouts and miso chan-chan mixture.

Cover with a lid and steam for 4–5 minutes or until cooked, depending on size of salmon.

When the salmon is cooked, remove the lid and add spring onion and butter. Put the lid back and on steam for a further 30 seconds or until spring onion is cooked to your preference.

Serve on plates or eat straight from the teppan.

You can include vegetables such as mushrooms, broccoli, parboiled pumpkin, cabbages, garlic chives, etc. with this dish: Cut four sheets of aluminium foil, approximately 40–50cm (15–20in) long. Place a portion of vegetables and spring onion topped with a salmon fillet in the centre of each. Pour miso mixture over the top. Fold edges of foil over securely to seal. Cook on the teppan covered with a lid, for 10 minutes. To serve, open foil and top with butter.

Salmon Chan-Chan Yaki

Skewered Snapper with Sansho

Serves 4

600g snapper fillets with skin
2 tablespoon sake
salt to taste
2 egg yolks
sansho powder to taste
2 tablespoons mirin
cooking spray

Cut snapper into 5mm (¼in) thick slices. Then cut these into smaller portions to make 12 pieces altogether, approximately 50g (1½oz) each.

Roll up each fillet. Skewer 3 rolls together as one serve.

Place skewers on a tray and sprinkle with sake and salt. Set aside.

Combine egg yolks, sansho powder and mirin in a small bowl.

Spray oil over rolls and cook snapper on the hibachi mesh, approximately a couple of minutes each side.

Brush egg mixture over the snapper and grill again. Be careful not to overcook snapper, as it will become tough.

Sansho powder has a very strong flavour so don't add too much.

Cubed Tuna

Serves 4

400g (14oz) tuna fillet (shoulder part is preferable)
4 tablespoons soy sauce
2 tablespoon mirin
2 tablespoons sake
4 tablespoons potato starch, kuzu powder or katakuriko
2 tablespoons vegetable oil
2 tablespoons butter
1 teaspoon sesame oil
1 teaspoon white sesame seeds
1 teaspoon aonori

Cut tuna into 2 x 2cm (¾in x ¾in) cubes. Marinate in soy sauce, mirin and sake in a bowl for 30 minutes.

Pat the tuna with a paper towel.

Place potato starch in a dish and add tuna to coat. Set aside for 5 minutes.

Heat teppan or barbecue hotplate and spread evenly with oil. Place tuna on hotplate and cook on all sides, taking care not to break up the cubes when turning.

Add butter and sesame oil. Garnish with sesame seeds and aonori.

When you buy tuna fillet, choose the shoulder part as this has firm flesh.
The tail and belly of tuna have veins and flake easily.

Whitebait with Yukari Mayonnaise

Serves 4

320g whitebait, rinsed
2 tablespoons mirin
salt to taste
2 tablespoons vegetable oil
4 tablespoons yukari mayonnaise (see page 189)
bamboo skewers

Thread whitebait onto bamboo skewers, approximately 10 fish per skewer. Place skewers on a tray or plate and sprinkle lightly with mirin and salt.

Heat a teppan, electric frying pan or barbecue hotplate and spread evenly with oil. Cook whitebait on both sides.

Spread with yukari mayonnaise and grill under the teppan.

Yukari is salted, dried red shiso.

Whiting with Green Tea Salt

Serves 4

4 whiting (150–200g/5–7oz each)
2 tablespoons mirin
½ tablespoon salt
½ tablespoon green tea powder
2 tablespoons soy sauce
4 lemon wedges
4 x 25cm (approximately 10in) metal skewers

Remove scales from whiting using scaler or knife. Make a slit on belly side and remove guts and gills. Rinse under running water.

Insert a metal skewer through the mouth of each fish along the length of the body, coming out at the tail, using a weaving motion.

Sprinkle with mirin and salt combined with green tea powder.

Heat barbecue grill. Insert the skewer tips between the grill slats so that the fish will cook in a standing position, head down.

When the skin becomes crispy, using a glove or a towel remove from the slats and serve on a plate.

Serve with lemon wedges and soy sauce as a dipping sauce on the side.

具、その他

Shellfish

その他

Shellfish

As with fish, it is important to purchase the freshest shellfish for your teppanyaki. There is a high risk of food poisoning from using deteriorating shellfish because of the poison they produce. Shellfish should have a fresh ocean smell and firm flesh.

Fresh molluscs such as squid, cuttlefish and octopus have a characteristic sliminess and a rubbery texture. Be sure they have a fresh ocean smell, but do not choose any that have a pinkish colour, as this is an indication that they are old.

The simple method used in teppan cooking allows for the flavours of shellfish to be fully appreciated, which is why live creatures such as lobsters, crabs and king prawns (shrimp) are used when possible. You may not have the opportunity to use live shellfish, but snap frozen shellfish are a suitable alternative, as they are frozen very quickly after being caught.

Combination Seafood Teppanyaki Platter

This simple recipe brings out the essential flavours of fresh seafood.

Serves 4

vegetable oil

1 carrot, cut into flower-shaped segments

4 thin slices zucchini (courgette)

4 x 5cm (1½ x 2in) pieces of leek, white part only

4 green king prawns (shrimp)

4 salmon fillets (50g/1½oz each) with skin

4 oysters in shells

4 tablespoons sake

4 tablespoons butter

salt and freshly grounded black pepper to taste

4 tablespoons mirin

4 lemon wedges

Heat a teppan, electric frying pan or barbecue hotplate and spread evenly with oil. Place carrot, eggplant and leek on one side and king prawns, salmon and oysters in the shell on the other side. Cook for 1 minute and turn all except oysters, cook for another minute.

Drizzle sake over vegetables and seafood and cook for 1 minute. Add butter, salt and pepper. Drizzle mirin over seafood and vegetables and cover with teppan lid to steam for 1 minute. When cooked, serve with lemon wedges.

I use vegetable cutters to cut carrot. You can use aspic cutters or other small decorative cutters or just slice. Prawns are cooked when the shells change to a reddish colour all over. Salmon fillets become white or light brown as they cook. Press lightly with finger or tongs to check if the flesh is soft or firm. If it is rare, the flesh will bounce back.

Crispy King Prawns

Serves 4

12 green king prawns (shrimp)

Chilli Marinade

2 fresh or dried red chillis

4 tablespoons soy sauce

1 glove garlic

1 tablespoon mirin

1 tablespoon sake

1 tablespoon caster sugar

2 tablespoons potato starch, kuzu powder or katakuriko

2 tablespoons butter

1 teaspoon roasted white sesame seeds

To prepare prawns, remove heads and set aside. Remove shells and discard, then devein prawns using a bamboo skewer.

To make chilli marinade, combine all the ingredients in a saucepan and mix well. Heat the sauce and allow to cool. Add king prawns to the mixture and marinate for 30 minutes.

Take out the king prawns and pat dry with paper towel. Keep the chilli marinade warm in the saucepan. Coat king prawns with potato starch in a dish.

Heat a teppan, electric frying pan or barbecue hotplate. Place butter on the heated plate and add the king prawns and heads. Cook prawns and heads on one side for about a minute, then turn them over and cook another minute. Press with a spatula.

Dip the prawns into the warm chilli mixture and cook both sides again.

Serve on individual plates sprinkled with sesame seeds

Butterfly King Prawns

Serves 4

8 green king prawns (shrimp)
2 tablespoons butter
1 tablespoon mayonnaise (wasabi, apple, umeboshi or miso—see pages 188–189)
20ml (¾fl oz) white wine

To prepare king prawns, remove heads and set aside. Remove shells and devein. With a sharp knife, make a slit down the back of each prawn and open up to make a butterfly.

Heat teppan or barbecue hotplate. Place butter on the heated plate and place prawns cut side down. Sprinkle with white wine.

Place a prawn head in the centre hole of each prawn and glaze with your choice of mayonnaise.

Grill under teppan burner for approximately 30 seconds.

Crab in White Sauce with Shiitake Mushrooms

Serves 4

pinch of salt
bowl of iced water
4 blue swimmer crabs (preferably female with roe)
1 tablespoon white wine
black pepper and salt
4 fresh small shiitake mushrooms, cleaned and scored with a cross
40g (1½oz) snow pea (sugar pea) sprouts

White Sauce

½ cup plain flour
4 tablespoon butter
1 cup milk

To make white sauce, gently melt the butter in a saucepan, then add flour, constantly stirring over a low heat until it has a crumbly texture. Gradually add warmed milk, stirring constantly until thickens. Remove from heat.

In a large pan, bring water to a boil and add a pinch of salt.

Prepare a bowl of water with ice cubes.

Cook crab for 1 minute then to the iced water. When crab is cool, remove and wipe dry with a paper towel. Remove carapace and set aside. Take out the flesh.

With a pair of cooking scissors, break the shells of the legs and take out the flesh. Gather flesh in a bowl and drizzle with white wine. Add white sauce and stir to combine. With a spoon, stuff the mixture into the upper crab shell.

Place the crab shell under heated grill for one minute then move to a heated teppan or barbecue hot plate for about 5 minutes. When cooked, top with shiitake mushrooms, cover with a lid and steam until mushrooms are soft.

Place crabs on a serving plate and garnish with snow pea sprouts.

You can add parmesan cheese or chopped parsley to the crab flesh before cooking.

Lobster with Mimosa and Nori Flakes

Serves 4

2 fresh lobster (approximately 500g/1lb each)
2 tablespoons sake
4 tablespoons butter
4 tablespoons soy sauce
2 tablespoons mirin
2 lemons, juiced
2 tablespoons mimosa (hardboiled egg, sieved or mashed)
1 tablespoon sliced nori

Cut lobsters in half lengthways.

Clean out head parts and rinse under running water. Place lobsters on a tray and sprinkle with sake.

Place butter on the cut sides and transfer onto a heated teppan, electric frying pan or barbecue hotplate.

Cook both sides.

Insert a fork into the edge of the lobster half-shells and remove the flesh. Swap the flesh from one shell to the other to cook the other side.

Sprinkle with soy sauce, mirin and lemon juice.

Serve garnished with mimosa and sliced nori.

You can buy sliced nori from Japanese grocery shops, or you can slice a sheet of nori.

Scampi with Olive Paste

Serves 4

8 scampi
½ tablespoon brandy or whisky
4 lemon wedges

Olive Paste

2 sun-dried tomatoes
140g (4 ½oz) pitted black olives
4 capers
2 preserved anchovies
2 tablespoons extra virgin olive oil
pepper to taste

To make olive paste, using a food processor, whiz chopped dried tomato, olives, capers and anchovies. Gradually add olive oil, and season with pepper.

Using a pair of cooking scissors, cut away the section of shell on the underside (belly) of the scampi from the tail to the head between the legs.

Insert a bamboo skewer from head to tail to make it straight.

Marinate the scampi in olive paste for about 30 minutes.

Transfer the scampi onto a heated teppan, electric frying pan or barbecue hotplate belly side up. Spread the remaining olive paste sauce over each scampi and cook for abut 5 minutes.

When cooked, pull out bamboo skewers. Using tongs to hold the scampi, carefully lift the flesh up from the shell, turn it over and place back in the shell. Return to hotplate, drizzle with brandy or whisky and flambé.

If using frozen scampi, defrost them first.
To flambé, use only a small amount of alcohol and do not
pour directly from the bottle. Light with a match.

Oysters with Green Tea Miso Sauce

Serves 4

2 egg whites
½ teaspoon caster sugar
1 tablespoon white miso paste
1 tablespoon mirin
1 teaspoon green tea powder
8 fresh Pacific oysters
1 stem leek, trimmed and shredded, soaked in water
1 lime, quartered

Place egg whites in a dry bowl. Add sugar, then make meringue-like sauce, whisking at full speed until stiff dry peaks form.

Mix white miso paste, mirin, and green tea powder well using a small whisk or fork. With a rubber spatula, add to the egg-white sauce and gently fold in with a wooden spoon. Set aside.

In a large bowl of lightly salted water, rinse oysters thoroughly and drain well.

Place a spoonful of sauce mixture on each oyster.

Place oysters on a heated teppan, electric frying pan or barbecue hotplate and grill until done—about a minute, but this depends on the size of the oysters.

When bubbles start to form, remove from hotplate and serve with shredded leek and lime wedges.

Spicy Pipis with Shiso

Serves 4

24 live pipis or clams
2 tablespoons butter
salt to taste
1 clove garlic, chopped
2 red chillis, de-seeded and chopped
salt
2 tablespoons white wine
4 shiso leaves, chopped, or 1 stem chopped lemongrass

Soak pipis in salted water for 1 hour to release any sand.
   Place butter on a heated teppan, electric frying pan or barbecue hotplate. Add pipis.
   Sprinkle pipis with garlic and chilli and stir.
Season with salt. Sprinkle with white wine. Cover with a lid and steam for 1 minute on high heat.
   Sprinkle with shiso or lemongrass and serve.

It is important to use live pipi; they are alive if they move when you touch them.

Scallops in Umeboshi Vinaigrette

Serves 4

1 teaspoon caster sugar
1 tablespoon umeboshi paste or 2 minced umeboshi
2 tablespoons rice vinegar
2 tablespoons water
2 tablespoons mirin
8 scallops with shells, guts discarded, rinsed in lightly salted water
2 tablespoons sake
10g (⅓oz) katsuobushi

Mix sugar, plum paste or minced umeboshi, rice vinegar, water and mirin in a small bowl.

Remove top shells of scallops and sprinkle each with sake.

Place scallops in shells on a heated teppan, electric frying pan or barbecue hotplate.

When the liquid in the scallop shells starts to bubble, release scallops from their attachments and put three scallops in each shell.

Spoon 1 teaspoon of plum paste mixture onto each scallop and grill for 1–2 minutes.

To serve, arrange the scallops in the shells with two on the bottom and one on top and sprinkle with bonito flakes

Scallops are available fresh in double shells, frozen in single shells, or frozen without shells. For this recipe it is important to use the shells.

Turban Shells with Miso and Shiitake in Bonito Dashi

Serves 4

4 dried shiitake mushrooms, soaked in water

2 tablespoons white miso paste

¼ cup bonito dashi (see page 179)

4 live turban shells

2 teaspoons butter

1 tablespoon sake

Drain shiitake mushrooms, squeeze out water and slice.

Mix white miso paste and dashi together.

Place turban shells on a heated teppan, electric frying pan or barbecue hotplate.

When the liquid in the shells starts to bubble, remove the flesh from the shell using a metal skewer, then place on a chopping board and set shells aside.

Cut off the shell cap from the flesh and chop the flesh. Remove the gut from the shell and place the chopped flesh inside the shells.

Add sliced shiitake, miso mixture, top with butter, then sprinkle with sake. Put the caps back on, place on hotplate and cook until just boiling.

Grilled Squid Stuffed with Fried Rice

Serves 4

4 small fresh squid or frozen squid tubes
spring onions, cut into 16 x 10cm (6 x 3½in) lengths
1 cup Fried Rice (see page 163)
2 tablespoons soy sauce
2 tablespoons mirin
1 tablespoon chopped fresh ginger
20g (¾oz) yukari powder
4 toothpicks or bamboo sticks

Clean the squid under running water and wipe dry with paper towel.

Score a criss-cross pattern on one side of each tube using a sharp knife.

Stuff each tube with 2 pieces of spring onion and fried rice and fasten the bottom with a toothpick.

Stir together the soy sauce, mirin and ginger and marinate the squid in this mixture for about 15 minutes.

Grill squid on a heated teppan, electric frying pan or barbecue hotplate, brushing occasionally with the marinade.

Sprinkle with yukari to serve.

Instead of fried rice, you may choose steamed rice or yakisoba.

Grilled Octopus with Soy Sauce

Serves 4

500g (1lb) baby octopus
salt for preparing octopus
bowl of iced water
2 tablespoons mirin

Soy Sauce Marinade

3 tablespoons soy sauce
1 tablespoon sesame oil
2 tablespoons caster sugar

Combine soy sauce, sesame oil and sugar in a small bowl and set aside.

Sprinkle salt over octopus and massage with fingers to remove sliminess.

Place in iced water and wash. Flip heads and remove the gut. Rinse well under running water and pat dry with paper towel.

Sprinkle with mirin.

Cook on the heated mesh of an hibachi or barbecue grill, brushing occasionally with soy sauce marinade.

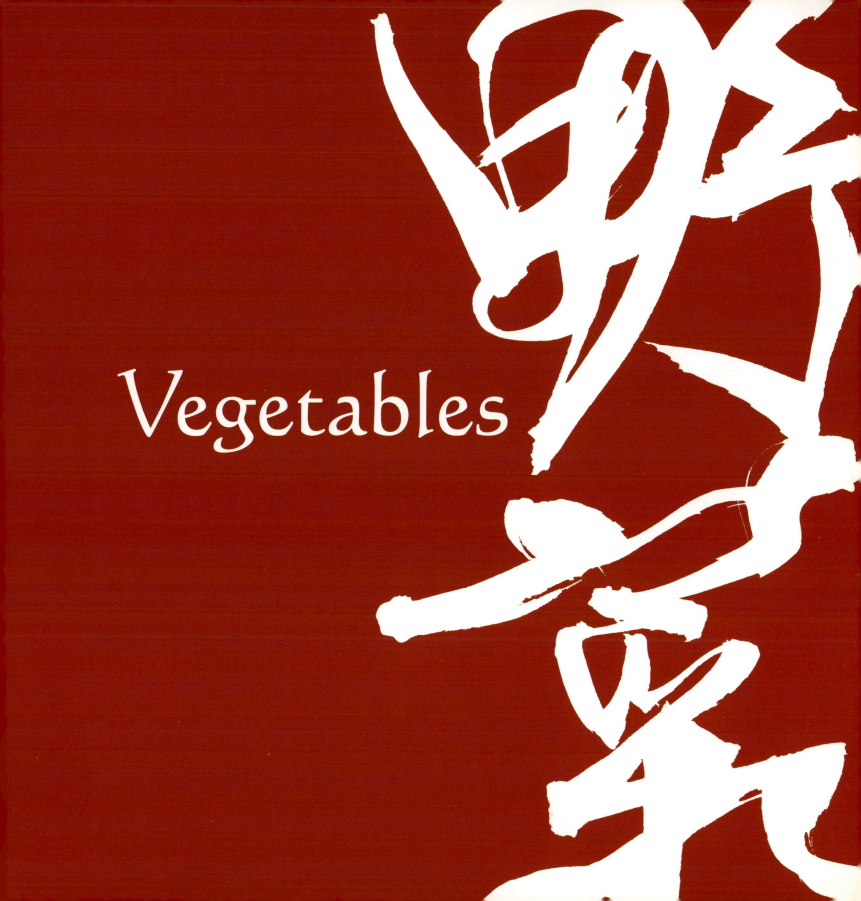

Vegetables

Vegetables

You can use almost any vegetable you find at the market in teppanyaki, but seasonal vegetables are always best.

Remember that some vegetables cook faster than others. Mushrooms, for example, don't take long to cook, so you have to work quickly. On the other hand, roots crops such as sweet potatoes take time to cook, so it's a good idea to partially cook them in the microwave before barbecuing.

Cooking vegetables on the teppan is quick and easy, and preserves the natural taste and texture of each ingredient. Simply grill in a little bit of oil and eat with your favourite sauce or dressing.

Tofu with Capsicum

Serves 4

8 pieces hard tofu (5 x 5 x 2cm/2 x 2 x ¾in thickness)
2 tablespoons katakuriko
2 tablespoons vegetable oil
½ small red capsicum (sweet peppers), seeded and diced
½ small yellow capsicum (sweet peppers), seeded and diced
½ small green capsicum (sweet peppers), seeded and diced
salt and pepper to taste
¼ cup mustard vinegar with miso puree
1 sheet nori, shredded

Miso Dressing

1 teaspoon English mustard
1 teaspoon rice vinegar
1 teaspoon mirin
2 tablespoons white miso
1 teaspoon caster sugar

To make the dressing, mix all the ingredients together.
Pat tofu dry using paper towel and coat with potato starch in a dish.
   Heat a teppan, electric frying pan or barbecue hotplate and spread evenly with oil.
   Cook tofu until an even golden colour on all sides. At the same time, cook capsicums lightly beside the tofu.
   Serve tofu on individual plates topped with capsicum and nori. Place dressing beside tofu.

Mushroom Combination

Serves 4

2 tablespoons soy sauce
¼ cup bonito dashi (see page 179)
1 tablespoon mirin
4 shiitake mushrooms
4 oyster mushrooms
4 shimeji mushrooms
1 bunch enoki mushrooms
2 tablespoons sake
1 tablespoon vegetable oil
2 tablespoons butter

Mix soy sauce, dashi and mirin in a small bowl.
Trim all mushrooms and place on a plate. Sprinkle with sake.
Drop oil on a heated teppan, electric frying pan or barbecue hotplate and cook mushrooms.
Add butter and stir gently.
Place on a serving plate and sprinkle with dashi mixture.

Eggplant Amiyaki

Serves 4

2 tablespoons light soy sauce
½ cup bonito dashi (see page 179)
1 tablespoon mirin
1 small brown onion, chopped and soaked in water
8 small Asian eggplants (aubergines)
4 teaspoons grated fresh green ginger
4 tablespoons bonito flakes

Combine soy sauce, dashi and mirin in a saucepan and cook over low heat for a couple of minutes. Set aside to cool.

Add drained onion to cooled sauce.

Grill whole eggplants on a mesh grill or barbecue grill until the skin starts to scorch.

Cut several slits in the skin of the eggplants and soak in a bowl of water with ice cubes, then remove skins.

Place eggplants in shallow bowls and spoon sauce over them.

Garnish with grated ginger and bonito flakes.

This dish is prepared in advance. It is served cold as an entrée.

Skewered Tomatoes

Serves 4

16 cocktail (cherry) tomatoes, blanched and peeled
320g bacon rashers, sliced into long, thin strips
2 tablespoons white wine
2 tablespoons butter
1 tablespoon roasted white sesame seeds
bamboo skewers

Roll a strip of bacon around each tomato.

Place 2 tomatoes on each bamboo skewer.

Sprinkle white wine over the tomatoes.

Drop butter on a heated teppan, electric frying pan or barbecue hotplate and grill tomatoes until the bacon becomes crispy.

Sprinkle with sesame seeds and serve.

Tomato and Daikon Salad with Dashi Dressing

Serves 4

2 medium vine tomatoes
200g (7oz) white daikon
100g (3½oz) mizuna leaves, soaked in water

Dashi Dressing

3 tablespoons bonito dashi (see page 179)
½ teaspoon sugar
2 teaspoons soy sauce
3 tablespoons rice vinegar
a few drops sesame oil
½ lemon, juiced

To make dashi dressing, combine all ingredients in a bowl and set aside.

Using a small knife remove the core from tomatoes and slice in half.

Cut one half of the tomatoes into small dice and slice the other half into 5mm (¼in) thin slices.

Soak diced tomato in dashi dressing.

Peel daikon. Using a mandolin, slicer or knife, slice daikon thinly, then cut slices into thin sticks.

Drain water from mizuna. Mix daikon with mizuna leaves.

Place mizuna and daikon on a plate and top with tomato slices.

Pour tomato-dashi dressing over the salad to serve.

お好み焼、麺

その他の

その他の鉄板焼

Pancakes, Noodles
and Other Teppanyaki Treats

Pancakes, Noodles
and Other Teppanyaki Treats

Outside of Japan, Teppanyaki is usually understood to be a meal of steak or seafood with vegetables cooked on a teppan hotplate. However, in Japan, two of the most popular teppanyaki meals are okonomiyaki and yakisoba noodles. Okonomiyaki, a type of pancake or omelet, originated in the Kansai area (around Osaka), so naturally there have been many restaurants in that area specialising in okonomiyaki for a long time, but these days they are found throughout Japan. They are usually very reasonably priced, and provide a tasty, filling meal.

Most Japanese tend to eat okonomiyaki at a restaurant or one of the many small food outlets, but in Kansai people commonly cook it at home using an electric hotplate.

Okonomiyaki Osaka-style

Serves 4

400g (14oz) cabbage, trimmed and chopped
4 eggs
4 tablespoons vegetable oil or lard
12 paper-thin slices pork, approximately 30g (1oz) each
okonomiyaki sauce (available from Japanese grocers)
Japanese mayonnaise
aonori powder

Okonomiyaki Pancake Batter

1 teaspoon katsuo dashi powder
250ml (8floz) water
200g (7oz) plain flour (weak flour is preferable)
10g (⅓oz) yamaimo powder or 80g (2½oz) frozen yamaimo, grated
1 teaspoon salt
400g (14oz)

To make pancake batter, combine dashi powder with water in a large bowl. Add other batter ingredients and whisk well.

In a small bowl, add ¼ cabbage, ¼ batter mixture and 1 egg.

Fold in with a spoon, do not mix.

Make pancakes one by one. On high heat, drop one tablespoon of oil on a heated teppan, electric frying pan or barbecue hotplate and pour on the mixture to make a pancake.

Place 3 pork slices on top of the pancake.

When bubbles appear on the surface, lower heat to medium and cook for 3 minutes.

Using two spatulas, turn the okonomiyaki pancake. Press pancake down firmly with spatula.

Break an egg beside the pancake on the hotplate. Using a corner of the spatula, break the egg yolk. Turn okonomiyaki pancake over onto the egg with a spatula. Push any leaking egg in towards the pancake to cook, keeping the shape of the pancake neat.

When egg is cooked, turn pancake over again. Brush with okonomiyaki sauce, dollop with mayonnaise and sprinkle with aonori.

Repeat this process to make three more pancakes. You can eat directly from the hotplate with chopsticks or serve on a plate.

Bonito-dashi powder is a convenient condiment for Japanese home cooking.
It can be used to flavour soups and many boiled dishes. It is available from Japanese or Asian grocers.
In Japan, fresh yamaimo is available in season, but outside of Japan it is available
in powdered or frozen form. Yamaimo makes okonomiyaki pancake firm but soft in texture,
with a mild flavour that does not dominate.
Instead of pork, you can use peeled king prawns, cuttlefish, oysters, cheese, chicken
or dried shrimps. Other ingredients, such as chopped benishoga (red pickled ginger),
chopped spring onion, mushrooms, corn kernels can also be added.
Japanese mayonnaise contains more egg yolk than Western varieties.

Another variation of okonomiyaki known as modanyaki (modern-style okonomiyaki), includes the addition of yakisoba noodles (Japanese-style egg noodle). To make, stir-fry noodles in a small amount of oil on the teppan beside the okonomiyaki. When the okonomiyaki is cooked, place noodles evenly on the pork (or whichever topping you have used), then break an egg in the centre of the noodles. Using a spatula, turn the okonomiyaki and cook through. When the egg is cooked, turn it over again and brush with sauce before serving.

Okonomiyaki Osaka-style

Okonomiyaki Hiroshima-style

Okonomiyaki Hiroshima-style

Serves 4

4 tablespoons vegetable oil

400g (14oz) savoy cabbage or green cabbage, trimmed and thinly sliced, soaked in water

16–20 very thin pork slices, approximately 30g (1oz) each

salt and black pepper to taste

200g (7oz) bean sprouts

40g (1½oz) bonito flakes

200g (7oz) egg noodles, boiled

4 tablespoons chicken stock

4 eggs

okonomiyaki sauce

aonori (dried green seaweed flakes)

4 stems spring onion, trimmed and chopped

Okonomiyaki Pancake Batter

pinch salt

1 teaspoon sake

1 teaspoon light soy sauce

½ teaspoon garlic powder or ½ clove chopped garlic

300ml (10fl oz) water

200g (7oz) plain flour

To make pancake batter, in a bowl, combine salt, sake, soy sauce, garlic and water. Mix well. Add flour and whisk. Rest in refrigerator for 2–3 hours.

Drain cabbage well.

Make pancakes one by one. Drop oil on a heated teppan, electric frying pan or barbecue hotplate. Pour a ladle of the mixture on the teppan, spreading into a circle using the bottom of the ladle to make a thin pancake. When the surface starts to dry, carefully turn it over with a spatula. When it is cooked, move it to the unheated side of the teppan or transfer it to a plate.

Place 4–5 slices of pork on the teppan and season with pepper and salt. Add bean sprouts and a pinch of bonito flakes, then 100g (3½oz) cabbage. Place pancake on the top to steam the cabbage.

At the same time, beside the pancake, place ¼ of the egg noodles and pour over 1 tablespoon chicken stock.

Using the teppan lid or a frying pan, press the pancake down firmly.

Break an egg on the teppan and cook until the egg white becomes dry. Place egg noodle on the egg. Using two spatulas place the pancake on the noodles and egg. Press down with lid or frying pan for 10 seconds then turn the pancake egg-side up.

Brush with okonomiyaki sauce and sprinkle with aonori and spring onion.

Repeat with remaining ingredients to make another three pancakes.

There are two types of plain flour; weak flour has less starch and strong flour contains. Weak flour works better in this batter.

Yakiudon

Serves 4

400g (14oz) udon noodles
4 tablespoons vegetable oil
16 thin pork slices (approximately 160g) or bacon
100g (3½oz) cabbage, trimmed and cut into approximately 3 x 3cm (1in x 1in)
80g (3oz) bean sprouts
salt and black pepper to taste
2 stems spring onion, trimmed and sliced diagonally
yakisoba sauce
aonori (dried green seaweed) flakes

Prepare udon noodles following instructions on the packet, drain well and keep warm.

Drop oil on a heated teppan, electric frying pan or barbecue hotplate. Add udon noodles and stir. At the same time, beside the udon, place sliced pork or bacon and stir well.

Place cabbage and bean sprouts on the top of the udon noodles. Season with salt and pepper. Stir all ingredients together for a couple of minutes. Sprinkle with yakisoba sauce and combine well. Serve on individual plates, sprinkle with aonori.

You can purchase udon noodle either frozen, vacuumed pack or dried.
If using dried udon, allow 300g and cook as per instructions on pack.
Yakisoba sauce is available from Japanese grocery shops.
You can use yakisoba noodles instead of udon.
For additional flavour, a few drops of sesame oil or chilli oil can be added
to the vegetable oil before cooking the noodles.

Yakisoba Omelette

Serves 4

    400g (14oz) yakisoba noodles, steamed
    4 tablespoons vegetable oil
    16 thin pork slices, approximately 30g (1oz) each
    8 eggs, beaten in a bowl
    100g (3½oz) cabbage, trimmed and cut into approximately 3 x 3cm (1 x 1in)
    salt and pepper to taste
    1 tablespoon Worcestershire sauce
    1 tablespoon tomato sauce
    4 tablespoons yakisoba sauce
    1 tablespoon Japanese mayonnaise

Steam yakisoba noodles and keep warm.

    Drop oil on a heated teppan, electric frying pan or barbecue hotplate.

    Place pork slices on teppan. Place cabbage on top and stir for 1 minute.

    Add yakisoba noodles and stir well, spreading noodles over the teppan.

    Season with salt and pepper and stir.

    Drizzle Worcestershire sauce and tomato sauce over noodles and stir again, pushing the noodles to one side of the teppan. On the other side, pour 4 equal amounts of beaten egg onto the hotplate, using a spatula to shape each into a separate omelet.

    Using two spatulas, place some yakisoba noodles on the front half of each omelet.

    Insert the spatulas underneath omelets from the back, without breaking the omelet, and fold over onto the part with noodles.

    Pour yakisoba sauce and mayonnaise onto the omelets before serving.

Gyoza Dumplings

Makes 16

Dumpling Mixture

100g (3½oz) Chinese or savoy cabbage, finely chopped

½ teaspoon salt

100g (3½oz) lean pork mince

1 tablespoon vegetable oil

½ teaspoon sesame oil

10 stems garlic chives, chopped or 1 stem spring onion, trimmed and chopped finely

1 tablespoon sake

½ tablespoon soy sauce

1 teaspoon caster sugar

1 teaspoon ginger juice (Grate green ginger and squeeze)

salt and white pepper to taste

16 round gyoza or gow gee wrappers

a bowl of water for sealing

½ cup water for steaming

vegetable oil

Dipping Sauce

4 tablespoon soy sauce

4 tablespoon rice vinegar

a few drops of sesame oil

a few drops of chilli oil

To prepare dipping sauce, combine all ingredients in a bowl and set aside.

Combine chopped cabbage and salt in a large bowl. Set aside until the cabbage wilts, approximately 30 minutes.

In another bowl, place pork mince and oils, and mix well with your hands.

Squeeze out water from cabbage and combine with chives, sake, soy sauce, sugar, ginger juice, salt and pepper.

Add pork to the cabbage mixture and mix well with your hands.

Holding gyoza wrapper in the palm of your hand, put about a tablespoonful of filling onto the centre of the wrapper.

Dip your index finger into water and wet in a line around the edge of the wrapper. Fold the wrapper over the filling. Seal the edges together by making small pleats on the top and pressing onto the back side. Repeat with remaining wrappers.

Drop oil on a heated teppan, electric frying pan or barbecue hotplate and place gyoza in rows of four.

Grill one side and turn over with a spatula.

Pour water over gyoza, and cover with lid to steam for 1–2 minutes.

Serve on a platter or individual plates with dipping sauce.

Takoyaki Octopus Balls

Takoyaki, mainly eaten as a snack between meals, is a dish of chopped octopus in batter cooked in ball shapes in an iron mould. The balls are eaten with a toothpick and served with special sauce. These traditional delicacies originated in Osaka, now the Mecca of takoyaki.
The takoyaki iron mould is hard to buy overseas, but is similar to a gem scone pan, so I suggest using an enamel or cast iron snail dish, gem scone or patty pan as a substitute.
Serves 4 (approximately 50 pieces)

250g (8oz) plain flour

1 tablespoon baking powder

3 eggs, beaten

1 litre bonito dashi (see page 179)

300 g octopus

30g (1oz) salt

bowl of iced water

salt or soy sauce to taste

4 tablespoons vegetable oil

30g (1oz) tenkasu or sakura ebi

3 tablespoons benishoga, chopped

takoyaki or okonomiyaki sauce, available from Japanese grocers

aonori

2 bamboo sticks

toothpicks to serve

Combine plain flour, baking powder, eggs and stock in a bowl, mix well and keep in the refrigerator.

To prepare octopus, rub with salt and cook in boiling water until it just changes colour. Soak in iced water until chilled. Chop into 1cm (½in) squares.

Heat the mould pan over gas, an hibachi or grill.

With a jug, gently pour the flour mixture into each well, filling to the rim. Put one piece of octopus, tenkasu and ginger on top of each ball. Cook over heat until the surface starts to set. Insert bamboo sticks gently under the edge of the ball, lift it up, and turn it over. This might take a bit of practice.

Once turned over, roll each ball around in its well to avoid over-cooking.

Transfer balls to a plate, pour on sauce and sprinkle with aonori. Pierce each ball with a toothpick and serve immediately while you continue cooking the remaining batter.

For the stock, bonito, anchovy or kelp stock is popular.
You can make it yourself or you may use instant stock powder.
Tenkasu is small, freshly fried batter pieces. It can be made by pouring a
fine stream of batter over a chopstick into a pan of hot oil, mixing it through the oil,
and removing as it floats to the surface. It should then be drained well on kitchen paper.
Commercial tenkasu is available from Japanese grocery shops.
For extra filling you may add a small amount of finely chopped cabbage,
spring onion or even grated cheese.

Fried Bean Curd Cheese Sandwich

2 teaspoons soy sauce

2 teaspoons mirin

1 teaspoon caster sugar

4 abura-age (fried bean curd)

8 cheese slices

2 stems spring onion, trimmed and chopped

a few drops vegetable oil or butter

shichimi to taste

Combine soy sauce, mirin and caster sugar in a bowl.

Cut bean curd in half.

Open up bean curd from the cut side, without tearing.

Gently slide cheese and spring onion inside the bean curd. Prepare all bean curds.

Brush both sides of bean curd with soy sauce mixture.

Drop oil on a heated teppan, electric frying pan or barbecue hotplate and grill bean curds on both sides over low heat.

With a knife, make a slit in the top of the bean curds so you can see the cheese.

Serve sprinkled with shichimi.

Fried Rice

Serves 4

600g cooked short grain or long grain rice
3 tablespoons vegetable oil
2 eggs, beaten
160g prawn (shrimp) meat
200g (7oz) bacon rashers, trimmed and chopped
1 stem spring onion, chopped
4 tablespoons fresh or frozen green peas, cooked
1 teaspoon powdered stock (chicken or vegetable)
salt to taste
pepper to taste

Cook the rice or if you are using leftover rice, warm it up in the microwave oven.

Drop oil on a heated teppan, electric frying pan or barbecue hotplate and add beaten egg, stirring until cooked.

Add prawn, bacon and spring onion and stir for 1 minute.

Add green peas and stir in.

Add warmed rice and stir about 2 minutes until well mixed.

Stir in stock powder, salt and pepper.

Place in a serving dish and serve warm.

Soy sauce or sesame oil can be added for extra flavour.

Crispy Rice

Serves 4

4 tablespoons soy sauce
2 tablespoons katakuriko
400g (14oz) cooked short grain rice
2 tablespoons mirin
2 teaspoons oil
1 tablespoon aonori

Mix soy sauce and potato starch together in a small bowl.

Drop oil on a heated teppan, electric frying pan or barbecue hotplate.

Place rice on the teppan, and using a spatula, press down all over to flatten it out and form a 3mm (1/8in) thick cake.

Sprinkle with mirin.

Using two spatulas, turn the rice and flatten again.

When rice becomes crispy, divide into quarters using a spatula.

Flatten each rice cake again. Brush with soy sauce and potato starch mixture on both sides then sprinkle with aonori.

Serve hot on individual plates.

Desserts

Desserts

Please remember that if you are making a dessert using the teppan after cooking meat or seafood products, be sure to remove all traces of meat and vegetables from the plate by wiping it well with a damp cloth.

These days—breaking with tradition—Japanese meals are becoming more adventurous and desserts more common. They tend to be light, however. With teppanyaki, being innovative is the key to success.

Grilled Seasonal Fruits

Serves 4

Slices of seasonal fruits—banana, oranges, pineapple, peaches, chestnuts—chopped into bite-sized pieces
Roasted cashew nuts, crushed
Roasted almonds, crushed
Spirit or liqueur, such as Grand Marnier

Grill fruit on a buttered teppan until carmelised. As a final touch flambé with spirit or liqueur then place in bowls and sprinkle with roasted nuts to serve.

Mint, Watermelon and Apple Sorbets

Serves 4

Mint

100g (3½oz) caster sugar

2 cups water

5g (¼oz) mint leaves, rinsed

Watermelon

100g (3½oz) caster sugar

¼ cup water

400g (14oz) watermelon , de-seeded

Apple

100g (3½oz) caster sugar

2 cups water

2 fuji apples, peeled and de-seeded (approximately 500g/1lb)

Make each sorbet flavour separately. Heat the caster sugar and water in a pan until sugar is dissolved. Let cool.

In a food processor, process the mint leaves and sugar mixture. Transfer to a container, cover and set in the freezer for 4 hours. Every 30 minutes, stir with a fork and return to the freezer.

Do the same with the apple and watermelon to make three separate flavours. Simply serve in individual bowls as a refreshing end to a teppanyaki meal.

Green Tea Pannacotta

Serves 4

  150ml (4½fl oz) thickened cream
  150ml (4½fl oz) milk
  5cm (2in) vanilla pod (split lengthways) or a drop of vanilla essence
  40g (1½oz) caster sugar
  1 teaspoon green tea powder, dissolved in 1 tablespoon hot water
  10g (¹/₃oz) gelatin powder, soaked in 100ml (3½fl oz) water
  8 pickled cherry petals
  4 moulds, lightly sprayed with a flavourless vegetable oil

Combine cream, milk, vanilla bean (if using) and sugar in a saucepan and cook over low heat, stirring occasionally until just boiling. Add green tea powder and vanilla essence, (if using).

Remove from the heat. Sprinkle gelatin over the the cream mixture, then stir continually until gelatin is dissolved.

Strain the custard through a sieve and pour into the moulds. Place in the refrigerator until set.

To serve, run a small knife around the mould to make the pannacotta easy to remove. Turn onto serving plates and garnish with cherry petals.

For the moulds, use $^1/_2$ cup plastic moulds, small ramekins or tea cups.
Pickled cherry petals are available from Japanese grocery shops.

Ice-cream Crepes

Serves 4

2 eggs, lightly beaten	100g (3½oz) caster sugar
1 teaspoon caster sugar	4 teaspoons butter
pinch of salt	4 scoops vanilla ice-cream
100ml (3½fl oz) milk	1 kiwi fruit, peeled and sliced
100g (3½oz) plain flour, sifted	4 strawberries, husked and halved
1 tablespoon butter, melted	1 tablespoon grand marnier, brandy or other liqueur
2 egg whites	4 mint leaves for garnish

Combine eggs, sugar and salt in a bowl. Gradually add milk and butter, beating to combine well.

Mix in flour. Set aside for 30 minutes.

To make froth, whisk egg whites in a clean, dry bowl, adding sugar one spoonful at a time until stiff, dry peaks form. Use either an electric food mixer or a whisk. Keep froth in the refrigerator until ready to use.

Heat a teppan or electric frying pan and drop on a teaspoon of butter. If you are using a non-stick teppan, use less butter. Pour on sufficient mixture for one crepe, spreading it into an even round shape with the bottom of a ladle or spoon. When the surface starts to set, turn it over with a spatula.

Place a few slices of kiwi fruit on the crepe, followed by a scoop of ice-cream. Put a spoonful of froth on top, then two halved strawberries. Sprinkle with liqueur and flambé.

Serve garnished with mint leaves.

Premixed or packet crepe or pancake mixture can be used for this recipe.
Once you have added the ice-cream you need to work quickly so that it doesn't melt with the heat of the teppan.
To flambé, use a ladle to sprinkle the liqueur rather than pouring straight from the bottle because the liqueur easily catches alight once on the heated teppan .

だし、ソース、ドレッシング

Stocks, Sauces and Dressings

Stocks, Sauces and Dressings

Dashi

Basic Japanese dashi stock is flavoured with katsuo, bonito and kombu (kelp). There is also a 'super dashi'; dashi with seasoning (soy sauce, mirin, etc.).

When you decide to do teppanyaki, I recommend you make dashi in advance. If you don't have time to make it, you can buy concentrated or powdered dashi from Japanese or Asian grocers.

Commercial katsuo dashi powder, also from Japanese or Asian grocers, is a convenient ingredient for Japanese home cooking. It can be used to flavour soups and many boiled dishes.

Bonito Dashi

Makes 2 litres (1 quart) of stock

2 litres (1 quart) water
4 x 4cm (1½in x 1½in) square dried kelp sheets, wiped dry
50g (1½oz) katsuobushi

Place kelp sheets in a large saucepan with water. Bring to the boil and cook another 2 minutes. Remove the kelp sheets. Put katuobushi in the pan and cook for about 5 minutes over low heat.

Prepare a bowl or pan covered with paper towel to use as a sieve. Sieve dashi stock. Store in refrigerator for up to 5 days. You can freeze it for up to a month but it is best freshly made.

Dipping Sauces

A dipping sauce adds extra flavour to simply cooked teppanyaki dishes. However, the key role of a dipping sauce is to enhance the flavour of the original ingredients, not to overpower them. There is a great range of sauces, and you should not limit yourself to those with a Japanese flavour. Other Asian and Western sauces provide suitable alternatives.
Serve dipping sauces in small serving bowls beside the main dish.

White Miso Dipping Sauce

Serves 4

¼ cup white miso paste
1 tablespoon mirin
1 tablespoon sake
1 tablespoon caster sugar

Mix all ingredients in a small saucepan and cook over low heat until sugar dissolves.
Serve warm.

Mattcha Miso Dipping Sauce

¼ white miso paste
1 tablespoon mirin
1 tablespoon sake
1 teaspoon green tea powder
1 tablespoon caster sugar

Mix all ingredients in a small saucepan and cook over low heat until sugar dissolves.
Serve warm.

Egg Miso Dipping Sauce

¼ cup white miso paste
1 egg yolk
1 tablespoon mirin
1 tablespoon caster sugar

Mix all ingredients in a small saucepan and cook over low heat until sugar dissolves. Serve warm.

Ponzu (Citrus Vinaigrette)

The name of this delicious vinaigrette comes from the Dutch word 'Pons', meaning citrus. You can buy commercial versions of ponzu from Japanese and Asian grocers. Traditionally, the juice of fresh yuzu (Japanese citrus) is used; however, outside of Japan, you can buy artificial yuzu juice or use fresh lime juice as a substitute.

¼ cup artificial yuzu juice or fresh lime juice
¼ cup rice vinegar or apple vinegar
¼ cup water
few drops vegetable or olive oil
few drops soy sauce

Mix all ingredients together in a small bowl.

Wasabi Vinaigrette

1 tablespoon wasabi paste
1 tablespoon caster sugar
1 teaspoon vegetable oil
1 tablespoon rice vinegar
¼ cup water
1 tablespoon mirin

Mix all ingredients together in a small bowl. This vinaigrette could also be used as a dressing.

Spicy Miso

1 stem spring onion, trimmed and chopped
1 tablespoon roasted white sesame seeds, grated
10g (¹/₃oz) Korean shredded dried chilli
¼ cup white miso
1 clove garlic, chopped
1 tablespoon mirin

Mix all ingredients together in a small bowl.

Sesame Soy Sauce

1 tablespoon nerigoma
1 teaspoon roasted white sesame seed, grated
¼ cup soy sauce
1 tablespoon sake
1 tablespoon caster sugar

Mix all ingredients together in a small saucepan and cook. Occasionally stir and remove from the heat when the sugar is disolved.

Sauces

The three basic sauces I introduce in this book are used extensively in teppanyaki barbecueing.
Teriyaki is a versatile sauce that works well with most ingredients.
Yakiniku sauce is especially good with pork, beef and chicken.
Jingisukan (Genghis Khan) sauce is wonderful with lamb.
Commercial versions are available from your local supermarket or Asian grocer.

Teriyaki Sauce
Makes 125ml (4 fl oz)

⅓ cup soy sauce
¼ cup water
50g (1½oz) rock sugar or caster sugar
¼ cup mirin

Combine soy sauce, water and caster sugar in a saucepan and cook until the sugar is dissolved.
Add mirin and simmer for 10 minutes.
This sauce can be used immediately or cooled and stored in the refrigerator for up to one month. Add some grated ginger before boiling, if you like.

A thicker teriyaki sauce can be made by adding 1 teaspoon potato starch or corn starch mixed with a little water before boiling, then stir well.

Yakiniku Sauce

Makes 125ml (4 fl oz)

1 onion, peeled
1 carrot, peeled
3 cloves garlic, peeled
10g (1/3oz) green ginger, peeled
1 fuji or pink lady apple, peeled and seeded
100ml (3½fl oz) water
1 tablespoon white roasted sesame seeds
1 tablespoon white miso
red chilli, to your preference
1 cup sake
1 cup mirin
100g (3½oz) caster sugar
4 cups soy sauce
2 tablespoons honey
1 teaspoon bonito dashi or 1 teaspoon chicken stock
a few drops sesame oil

In a food processor, whiz onion, carrot, garlic, ginger, apple and water. Then add sesame seeds, miso and chilli if using, then whiz.

Place sake and mirin in a large saucepan and bring to the boil. Add sugar and soy sauce.

Transfer the mixture into the saucepan and cook over the medium heat as stirring.

Add honey and stock. Cook for 20 minutes over low heat. Drop in sesame oil and cook another 5 minutes.

Let cool and store in refrigerator for up to 2 weeks.

Jingisukan (Genghis Khan) Sauce

Makes 200ml (6½ fl oz)

1 garlic clove, grated
1 small piece of green ginger, grated
½ brown onion, peeled and grated
1 green apple, peeled and grated
½ cup water
²/₃ cup soy sauce
3 tablespoons vegetable oil
1 tablespoons sesame oil
1 tablespoon ground white sesame seeds
2 tablespoons honey or caster sugar
1 tablespoon mirin
1 tablespoon sake
1 lemon, juiced

Put garlic, ginger, onion, apple, water and soy sauce in a saucepan, bring to the boil. Add vegetable oil, sesame oil, sesame seeds and honey.

Cook for 10 minutes, occasionally stirring over low heat.

Add mirin and sake and cook for a further 5 minutes. Add lemon juice and stir for a couple of minutes, then remove from the heat.

Cool down before using. Store in refrigerator for up to 1 month.

If using as a marinade the sauce can be prepared the day before if desired.

Dressings and Mayonnaise

In Japan, dressings are similar to French dressings—based on oil and vinegar with added flavours. Japanese soy sauce, fresh ginger juice, sesame oil and yuzu (Japanese citrus) are popular ingredients. Dressings are used on salads or served with barbecued meats and vegetables cooked on the teppan.

Recently, mayonnaise is used, mixed with other ingredients such as herbs, wasabi and miso paste. Mayonnaise is used on toast instead of cheese. It is quite tasty! You can buy Japanese mayonnaise from Japanese or Asian grocery shops, or you can just use a commercial or homemade variety from your supermarket.

The dressings and mayonnaise recipes here will store for up to a week in a sealed jar in the refrigerator.

Green Apple Mustard Dressing

Serves 4

1 teaspoon vegetable oil

1 granny smith apple, peeled and grated

1 teaspoon English mustard

1 teaspoon rice vinegar

¼ cup water

1 teaspoon caster sugar

1 teaspoon mirin

black pepper to taste

Mix all ingredients together in a small bowl.

Ume Shiso Dressing

1 teaspoon olive oil
1 teaspoon rice vinegar
1 teaspoon caster sugar
1 teaspoon mirin
1 tablespoon bainiku
½ teaspoon yukari
¼ cup water

Mix all ingredients together in a small bowl.

Wasabi Mayonnaise
Serves 4

4 tablespoons Japanese mayonnaise
$1/8$ tablespoon wasabi paste

Stir ingredients together thoroughly.

Apple Mayonnaise
Serves 4

4 tablespoons Japanese mayonnaise
1 small Granny apple, peeled and grated
salt to taste

Stir ingredients together thoroughly.

Plum Paste (Umeboshi) Mayonnaise

Serves 4

  4 tablespoons Japanese mayonnaise
  1 tablespoon bainiku

Stir ingredients together thoroughly.

Miso Mayonnaise

Serves 4

  4 tablespoons Japanese mayonnaise
  1 tablespoon white miso paste

Stir ingredients together thoroughly.

Yukari Mayonnaise

  4 tablespoons Japanese mayonnaise
  1 teaspoon yukari powder

Stir ingredients together thoroughly.

Index

About the Author

Hideo Dekura was born in Tokyo and started his training in his family's two restaurants. Here he learnt the principles of sushi and kappou-ryōri food preparation, cooking and presentation. At the same time he studied the philosophy of Chakaiseki (the cuisine of the tea ceremony), Teikanryu Shodo (calligraphy), Ikenobō-Ryûseiha (flower arrangement) and Hōchō Shiki (the ceremony of the cooking knife) from Iemoto-Shishikura Soken-sensei under the authority of Shijyōshinryû.

Since 1974 Hideo has lived in Sydney, where he set up the event catering company Japanese Functions of Sydney. His Culinary Studio Dekura provides a base for his food consulting work and lectures on Japanese cooking.

In 2007, the Japanese government presented Hideo with an award for making a significant contribution to the promotion of Japanese food and cooking.